"Do not blame her," Mr. Liffy told him.
"Just get to school on time, do you hear?"
"Yes, sir."
Chris sighed. He was worn out.

There was a snicker from the back of the room. It was Harry.

Harry and his friends kept giving Chris a hard time.

Staying Together

Written by
Jill Atkins

Illustrated by
Miguel Díaz Rivas

Published in 2026 by
Norwood House Press
2544 Clinton Street
Buffalo, NY 14224

Printed in the United States of America

Library of Congress Cataloging-in-Publication Data:
Names: Atkins, Jill (Children's author).| Rooney, Anne, author. | Díaz Rivas, Miguel, illustrator.
Title: Staying together / written by Jill Atkins, illustrated by Miguel Díaz Rivas. Panda school / by Anne Rooney.
Description: Buffalo, NY : Norwood House Press, 2026. | Series: Phonics all-stars: phase 5b
Identifiers: ISBN 9781978578593 (pbk.) | ISBN 9781978578609 (library bound) | ISBN 9781978578616 (ebook)
Subjects: LCSH: Reading–Phonetic method–Juvenile literature. | English language–Phonetics–Juvenile literature. | People with disabilities–Juvenile fiction. | Families–Juvenile fiction. | Pandas–Juvenile literature.
Classification: LCC LB1573.3 A796 2026 | DDC 372.465–dc23

CPSIA compliance information: Batch #CW26NHP: For further information contact Norwood House Press at 1-800-237-9932.

Chris dashed into school.

“Late again,” said Mr. Liffy. “What’s the excuse today?”

“Sorry, sir,” muttered Chris. “My sister, Charlene ... ”

In chemistry, Harry sent Chris little notes. The notes told him that something bad might happen to him.

Chris slipped out of school as soon as the bell sounded.

He ran to Charlene's school.

Charlene was waiting with her teacher, Mrs. Smith.

"Is everything all right?" Mrs. Smith asked.

Chris nodded, then took Charlene's hand and left.

Life was tricky for Chris.

He was late for school every day.

He had no friends – and Harry kept pestering him.

But he had to keep going.

At the end of the week,
Mr. Liffy asked to see Chris.

"Not now," said Chris.

At Charlene's school, Mrs. Smith asked him to wait.

"Not now," said Chris, as he led Charlene away.

The next day at school, Chris was sent to see Mrs. Philips.

"I have discussed this with Mr. Liffy and Mrs. Smith," she said. "Now, what's it all about, Chris? You can tell me."

Chris looked at her, feeling tears welling up.

"Sit down," said Mrs. Philips. "Let's see if we can sort something out."

Chris sighed. It was all too much.

"My mom is in a wheelchair," he said. "I feed her and Charlene. I do everything for them."

"I see," said Mrs. Philips. "Thank you for telling me. You are very brave, but you cannot carry on like this. I will need to tell people. They can help you."

"No!" pleaded Chris, thinking about Harry's notes. "They will split us up!"

"We will do the best we can," said Mrs. Philips.

His tears welled up again.

People came to see Chris at home.

"Helpers will come daily," said a man. "That will allow the family to stay together."

"Thank you," sighed Chris.

"No," said the man. "It's thanks to you."

Panda School

By Anne Rooney

Giant Pandas inhabit the bamboo forests of China.

With their cute faces and thick, furry ears, they look so soft and cuddly.

Yet they are powerful animals and can be a danger to you!

The panda's white face and belly hide it against winter ice.

Its dark parts blend into the forest shadows.

Pandas are now in danger, as there are few unspoiled places left for them.

People are just too willing to slice down the bamboo forests and replace them with farmland.

Pandas can now be found in six mountain ranges, in three parts of China.

At last, increasing concern for pandas is giving them the opportunity to survive.

In the race to save pandas, the cubs are reared by hand in safe places and then set free.

Trained assistants look after the babies in panda playgroups!

Raising panda babies might be the nicest job you could have. Just think – you get to embrace a panda!

Newborn pandas are tiny. They are only as heavy as a bar of soap.

The mom is huge – she is a thousand times larger than her baby!

When babies are born, they are pink and hairless. After a while, their fur starts to grow.

In the first stage, white fuzz grows, making grey bands in places that will later be black.

They soon turn into fluffy, cute little cubs. All traces of pink skin are hidden.

To begin with, pandas just drink milk. Once their second set of teeth have emerged, the cubs can eat bamboo.

The space in the playgroup is arranged so that the babies get many chances to play as they grow larger.

The assistants get the cubs to stand upright, clamber, roll, and race up and down.

The pandas engage with their assistants too. Hugs please the pandas and the assistants!

The panda playgroup is a safe place for the cubs.

It has doctors to help sick pandas, and there is even a panda school! The pandas pick up skills that they will need once they are in the wild.

At last, the pandas are released into the forest.

Everyone hopes that they will feel at home and have panda babies of their own one day.